KIMBERLY RODRIGUEZ

GETTING PERSONAL
WITH GOD

Getting Personal With God

All rights reserved. This book or any parts thereof may not be reproduced in any form, stored in any retrieval system, or transmitted in any form by any means – electronic, mechanical, photocopying, recording or otherwise – without prior written permission from the author or publisher. If you would like permission to use material from the book, please contact empressroyalepublishing@gmail.com.

Copyright © 2023 by Kimberly Rodriguez
Cover design by Empress Royále Publishing
Edited by Theastarr Valerie

Scriptures taken from the Holy Bible, New International Version®, NIV®. Copyright © 1973, 1978, 1984, 2011 by Biblica, Inc.™ Used by permission of Zondervan. All rights reserved worldwide. www.zondervan.com The "NIV" and "New International Version" are trademarks registered in the United States Patent and Trademark Office by Biblica, Inc.™

Empress Royále Publishing
"Everything tells a story…"
1-646-468-3114

Cover photo by Zbynek Pospisil from iStock

ISBN 9798985358346

Acknowledgments

God, I thank You for Your grace and this opportunity to write my book. I am humbled because of what You've been doing in my life. It is a privilege knowing Jesus Christ as my Lord and Savior.

> "Yet to all who did receive him, to those who believed in his name, he gave the right to become children of God—children born not of natural descent, nor of human decision or a husband's will, but born of God."
>
> *John 1:12-13*

I would also like to thank my best friend for support, faith, and encouragement in this process.

To my mom, thank you for supporting me in everything I do.

To those who would have encouraged me in this journey, thank you.

Note From the Author

I pray that everyone who reads this book will have a transforming experience. May you grow in God, encounter Him like never before, and be an encouragement to those you come in contact with (believers and unbelievers). There is no one that God is unable to save...

"I revealed myself to those who did not ask for me; I was found by those who did not seek me. To a nation that did not call on my name, I said, 'Here am I, here am I.'"

Isaiah 65:1

Jesus Christ is waiting for you and it is never too late to experience him. Fight for your relationship with God because this is one relationship that is worth it. Never stop seeking God.

Foreword

For the few years I've known Kimberly, I found her to be a bubbly, caring, resilient, multi-talented Christian woman who has a growing passion for the things of God. She's not afraid to admit her faults and be vulnerable to those close to her. Her ability to learn from her past mistakes and use those experiences to help both children and young adults astounds me. She has grown spiritually and I know God will use her mightily to impact those in her sphere of influence.

As you read through the pages of this book, allow God to minister to you by each written word. These words were received directly from the Holy Spirit because God had you specifically in mind. You will be encouraged by the testimonies shared and you may sense that yearning for a deeper intimate relationship with your Heavenly Father. I fully endorse each page written in this book because I know it comes from a place of authenticity and humility; so many will encounter that rich intimacy of God's love.

~Vernoma Joseph

Preface

This book was **inspired** by the prompting of the Holy Spirit. A few of my friends encouraged me to pen my thoughts.

I became a Christian at the age of 15. This experience led me to become a diligent reader of God's word. Whenever God spoke, I would *write* it down in my journal: verses, previous messages from God, or reminders of His words.

I was **eager** to know this God of the Bible and the God that I heard people speak so intimately about. It was this eagerness that sparked my desire to learn all that I could about who He is.

I hope I'm not the only person that did this, but at first, I would randomly *flip* open the Bible and whatever page it landed on I would say that **_God talked to me_**.

At times it would land on Psalms, Isaiah, or 1 Kings, etc. Although when I read it, something didn't feel right in jumping from one book to the other like that. Until someone told me to start with the New Testament gospels (Matthew, Mark, Luke, and John).

So, I started by reading the New Testament.

This journey to know Jesus Christ was not as easy as I believed. In fact, it was quite difficult for me. The difficulty stemmed from my uncertainty regarding how God would even speak to me. I wondered if I would literally **_hear_** His voice.

At first, I was nervous and thought, *If I hear God's voice, it would make me a crazy person…*

Whenever I read the Bible, many thoughts *circulated* my mind and I would become frustrated. There was a **block**; I heard nothing and received no insight from the text.

One day I decided to change my pattern. I prayed.

"God, I have been trying to read the Bible and get to know You and all that You did for me by sending Your son Jesus Christ to save me... But I am not hearing anything from You."

At that moment the Holy Spirit quietly replied, *"How can you hear me if you have clouded your mind with all these thoughts?"*

I realized that this made complete sense.

How could I expect to hear Him speak if my mind would not shut up?

The next day I got up at 5:00 (my usual devotional time) and I opened the Bible. **Nothing happened...**

I went away that morning with knowledge of the story, but I didn't know how to apply it to my life. Knowing the story was just the **beginning**.

The next morning, I woke up before my usual time and I prayed...

"Heavenly Father, my name is Kimberly and I have accepted your son Jesus Christ in my life. I read that the Holy Spirit is given to those who have accepted Jesus Christ. I believe that I have the Holy Spirit inside of me now. I don't have much to say. But I want to know You, I want to hear You, I want to be in Your presence and I never want to leave. I just want to hear from You. My ears are open, my heart is open, and please

open my eyes so that when I read Your word, I can see what You are saying to me today and every day. Thank You in Jesus' name. Amen."

That morning everything changed because I gave God **FULL CONTROL** of my time spent in His presence.

After that moment, I would just sit and welcome the presence of God in my time of devotions. Whenever I spent time with God, I would reread my notes to remind myself of what He said. I also read it throughout the day so that I would not forget His word.

1 Chronicles 22:19

Getting Personal With God

A relationship with God is crucial in a Christian's life. It is like spending time with your family or best friend.

God is never far. He is actually closer than your next breath.

When I became a new believer in Jesus Christ, spending time with God always seemed weird. At first, I felt crazy because I was speaking to someone invisible. But let me tell you, I felt His presence and it was always strong.

Even in the times where I did not feel His presence, I just knew He was there. That gave me hope.

Jesus set an example for us by going away to spend time with His Father. Our devotional life is like a tree, the more we water and nurture it, the more it grows and produce fruit.

Think About It: We eat physical food and drink water so that our bodies are nourished, can grow, and be strong. If we do not eat for a day or days, we become weak, our lips become dry, and our stomach gurgles.

*This concept also applies spiritually: our spirit can become weak and vulnerable without spiritual **food**.*

> "Man shall not live on bread alone, but on every word that comes from the mouth of God."
>
> Matthew 4:4

When we are weak it is easy for us to fall into temptation and be vulnerable to the enemy.

SPIRITUAL FOOD IS NECESSARY FOR YOUR SPIRITUAL GROWTH.

Quality time with God is more than a ritual. It is more than repeating a prayer or reading a book from the Bible.

It is about:

- Prayer
- Meditation
- Worship
- Giving God undivided attention during your devotions.

- Lying down at night, giving God thanks for keeping you throughout the day.
- Setting aside time for God daily
- Waking up early in the morning to speak to the Creator.

THIS TIME OF UNDIVIDED ATTENTION REQUIRES NO:

Cell phones

Laptops

Tablets

Food

It's just you and God.

The day belongs to God.

Can you see it like that?

God woke you up. He is the one that makes you breathe. Don't you think that He deserves us spending time with

Him when we wake up? I believe that God gives us His undivided attention.

> *"You will seek me and find me when you seek me with all your heart."*
> **Jeremiah 29:13**

In the quietness of our heart, that's when we seek God. Our heart yearns for something more.

Have you ever wanted something so badly that you'd do anything to get it? Or when pursuing an opportunity, you give it your all?

This is how you should pursue God...

- Seeking Him daily
- Reading His word
- Listening to Him
- Learning who He is
- Talking with Him
- Getting involved in ministry
- Asking others about Him

As recorded in the Bible, Jesus took time to be with His Father.

> "After he had dismissed them, he went up on mountainside by himself to pray. Later that night, he was there alone..."
> **Matthew 14:23**

He sent the crowd away.

No distractions

No phone

No TV

No music

Just Jesus and His Father.

At the end of the day, it is just you and God. I know we live in a technological generation and our Bible is on our phones or laptops, but let me encourage you to get a physical Bible so that you can highlight scripture verses as you read. *You can always go back to these verses.*

If you could see my Bible... it is colorful and has notes at the side.

Reading the Bible or having devotions is a discipline that we all have to develop. It's not easy to wake up earlier when you have a family to take care of, school to attend, or work to get ready for... Some of us do these things in the late evening. We **all** have responsibilities.

There are times that I sleep extra or attend to my chores first instead of praying or spending time with God and it **does** affect my day.

Moses realized that he needed God for every step of the way in his life. As believers, we must see it like that: realizing that we need God every second of the day.

> "Then Moses said to him, 'If your Presence does not go with us, do not send us up from here.'"
> Exodus 33:15

Can we as Christians or new believers be determined to pray and say, *"God if your presence does not go with me today, I am not going?"*

Going without the protection of God is something we never want to experience.

God, if You are not sending me...
I am not going.
If You say I should not take a particular job...
I will not take it.
If You say *do not pursue someone or something...*
I won't.

THIS IS SURRENDER.

THIS IS SEEKING GOD IN EVERY AREA OF YOUR LIFE.

God desires total surrender from us in ministry, finances, relationships, marriage, and our jobs.

In 2017, I graduated from UWI and was going to pursue my Bachelors in Education. I was denied, but got accepted to do a Bachelors in Communication Studies. Even though it wasn't what I wanted to do, I accepted it because my other friends were moving forward to do their bachelor's and I didn't want to be left behind.

I honestly knew God was leading me to take a break and focus on ministry and find out the different options for schooling, but I refused and that year I failed every single course. Not because I wasn't capable, but **God had been stirring me in a different direction.**

So, I had to forcefully call the school and put a hold on my account. There was no other option: I had to **take a break and figure out what God wanted me to do**.

For the next eight months I cried out to God for direction. From that year I always ask God's guidance for my life. *Hopefully, I learned my lesson.* God always look for those with obedient hearts.

There were times where I was so desperate for God, that I would go to bed crying...

I would kneel down by my bed and ask God for **one more encounter** with Him.

Even when everything feels stagnant, I trust that God is working things out for me.

When our life is not going as planned, will we be desperate and cry out to Him? I have learned to trust God when things are going well and trust Him when things are not going as planned.

My Prayer...

Direct me

God change me

I can't do this without You

I need more of You

I need to be where Your presence is

I need to be where You want me to be

I NEED YOU GOD

We live in a world where everything is a distraction. Our focus is on <u>carnal things</u> and not God.

Moses went up into the mountains so that God could speak to him away from the ***noise*** of life.

As we go through life, sometimes our day gets busy and we can become frustrated, distant, lost, and distracted with daily activities; whether it's for family, church, school, or work.

Eventually, we are so drained that we forget to run to the One (God) who can strengthen us. The One who has our best interest at heart. **Get rid of the noise...**

"But when you pray, go into your room, close the door and pray to your Father, who is unseen. Then your

Father, who sees what is done in secret, will reward you."
Matthew 6:6

Recently, my prayers have been full of tears... I need God so much.

 *Let's look at two stories from the Old Testament...*

EXODUS 14: MOSES AND THE ISRAELITES LEFT EGYPT AND THEY REACHED THE RED SEA, THEIR ENEMIES PURSUING THEM WITH NO ESCAPE... BUT GOD.

DANIEL 6: A YOUNG MAN WHO WAS PUT IN CHARGE OF MANY THINGS AND THE KING SHOWED HIM FAVOR. DANIEL HAD A SITUATION WHERE HE WAS BEING THROWN INTO THE LION'S DEN. NO ONE COULD HAVE SAVED HIM, NOT EVEN THE KING... BUT GOD.

I encourage you to read these stories and see how God showed up for the Israelites when it seemed like there was no way of escape. God opened up a way for them.

I believe that God hears when we whisper to Him the thoughts that overwhelm us. The tears that we cry when there are no words, are our prayers too.

Things can be tough and overwhelming at times and it can seem like forever. The question plagues your mind... **When will this stop?**

You just lost your job, or your mom; there's no unity in the family, you had an accident or an injury... Sometimes you can feel like it's one thing after the next and you're like GOD **I need a break**.

There are times when it feels like He is far.

Let me assure you that He is right there, riding through the storms with us. He promises that He *will never leave us nor forsake us*. God cannot and will not break a promise.

"Come to me, all you who are weary and burdened, and I will give you rest. Take my yoke upon you and learn from me, for I am gentle and humble in heart, and you will find rest for your souls. For my yoke is easy and my burden is light."

Matthew 11:28-30

Try it today
Give it all to God; everything that is bothering you
Surrender it all to Him

Taste and see that the Lord is good
See what God can do in and through your life…

"Taste and see that the LORD is good…"
Psalm 34:8

That was exactly what I did because I wanted more.

> **"Be still, and know that I am God..."**
> **Psalm 46:10**

Be still in the presence of God. It is not always about us talking to God and telling Him what our problems are. Although there is nothing wrong with that, we need to remember that God wants to speak to us.

Sometimes I have a problem with listening because I love to talk. And nothing is wrong with that, but I had to learn to allow God to speak to me.

This reminds me of Elijah in 1 Kings 19:11-13. Three elements were mentioned in this story:

- A powerful wind
- An earthquake
- Fire

Elijah was looking for God to speak to him through one of those elements, but God came with a whisper.

Sometimes we look for God to shout, but He comes and He whispers.

Be still and know He is God.

THE ONLY WAY THAT WE CAN HEAR GOD IS IF WE ARE *STILL* AND <u>SILENT</u> IN HIS PRESENCE.

Turn off our thoughts

Quiet our hearts

Open our ears to hear Him speak

We live in a world where it is hard to be still for a few minutes because distractions are always around.

David said, *"I wait for the LORD, my whole being waits, and in his word I put my hope."* Psalm 130:5

"Yes, my soul, find rest in God; my hope comes from him."
Psalm 62:5

Being with God and setting aside that time strengthens you:

Physically

Emotionally ✔

Spiritually ✔

Mentally ✔

> "So I turned to the Lord God and pleaded with him in prayer and petition, in fasting, and in sackcloth and ashes."
>
> **Daniel 9:3**

FASTING:

- Is an integral part of our Christian walk.
- Allows us to abstain from what we normally eat or do.
- Develops intimacy with God.
- Helps us go deeper in God.

In the Bible we see various accounts of fasting, but the highlight was to **seek God**.

I believe fasting is a form of self-discipline.

MOSES WAS SEEKING GOD'S WISDOM AND DIRECTION.

"Moses was there with the Lord forty days and forty nights without eating bread or drinking water. And he wrote on the tablets the words of the covenant—the Ten Commandments."
Exodus 34:28

REPENTANCE AND FASTING SHOWS THAT DESIRE TO RETURN TO GOD WITH ALL YOUR HEART.

> "'Even now,' declares the LORD, 'return to me with all your heart, with fasting and weeping and mourning.' Rend your heart and not your garments. Return to the LORD your God, for he is gracious and compassionate, slow to anger and abounding in love, and he relents from sending calamity."
>
> Joel 2:12-13

THE HOLY SPIRIT GUIDES US DURING FASTING.

We've all had experiences where it seems like our life isn't going anywhere. You question whether to go ⬅ left or ➡ right.

During fasting, when we shut out all the noise and we're in tune with the Holy Spirit, He gives us specific instructions on how to proceed. This applies to every area of our lives: *personal, ministry, school, work...* just like Moses seeking wisdom and direction from God.

FASTING SHOULD BE BETWEEN YOU AND GOD.

Our heart condition is broadcasted during this time. Fasting isn't just about *giving up food,* it is a demonstration of our hunger for more of God, the only One who can satisfy our soul.

FAST FOR SPIRITUAL GROWTH AND A PERSONAL RELATIONSHIP WITH GOD.

"Is not this the kind of fasting I have chosen: to loose the chains of injustice and untie the cords of the yoke to set the oppressed free and break every yoke?"
Isaiah 58:6

I have seen God answer my prayers through prayer and fasting not just with material things, but He...

- Builds my character
- Increases my faith in Him
- Strengthens me when I am weak
- Picks me up when I fall
- Humbles me enough to forgive those who have wronged me
- Guides me in ministry, school, and my personal life

At the beginning of every year my best friend and I would journal things we want to see happen spiritually in our lives. For the past 5 years it was **"A deeper relationship with God"**, **"Let your WILL be done"**. Now this can mean anything. There has always been that thirst to have more of God even when He disciplines us as His children.

As the year went by my daily prayer was to have a deeper relationship with God. I may not have understood the true purpose of all the things that I went through, but I know that *God, You had a plan for it.*

For every obstacle, storm, heartbreak, setback; for every time I felt like giving up, every time I strayed away from God, every time my heart was hard towards God; for every time it brought me to break... every lesson taught me that I cannot do it on my own... God had a plan!

Mold me God I pray, so that I can be who You want and have called me to be. God, I want to be so caught up in You and building Your kingdom that I forget about the cares of the world. ALL I want to do is please You.

> "I proclaimed a fast, so that we might humble ourselves before our God and ask him for a safe journey for us and our children, with all our possessions... 'The gracious hand of our God is on everyone who looks to him, but his great anger is against all who forsake him.' So we fasted and petitioned our God about this, and he answered our prayer."
> Ezra 8:21-23
> **FASTING BRINGS HUMILITY.**

Why do you fast? Are there things that you need to fast and pray about?

_____

_____

_____

_____

_____

_____

Meditation

A very important part of getting personal with God is reading His word. Reading the Bible is essential in getting to know God and who He is.

WHEN READING THE BIBLE, YOU LEARN ABOUT GOD'S...

CHARACTER

LOVE

SACRIFICES

MERCY

GRACE

PROVISION

PROTECTION

DISCIPLINE

"Keep this Book of the Law always on your lips; meditate on it day and night, so that you may be careful to do everything written in it."
Joshua 1:8

> "But whose delight is in the law of the Lord, and who meditates on his law day and night."
> Psalm 1:2

Meditate: *to focus one's mind for a period of time in silence or setting aside time every day to write or think deeply about something.*

Reading His word tells us who He is.

I always believed that God is concerned about every detail of our lives. Think about a parent or someone who cares for you; whatever you do, they want to hear all about it. They want to hear the good, bad, and everything in between...

Although God knows everything about you, He is still interested in hearing from you about it.

God is concerned about your fears and interests.

God sees us.

Genesis 16:13 captures this perfectly. *"'You are the God who sees me,' for she said, 'I have now seen the One who sees me.'"*

God sees our battles; He sees and knows our inmost being. He knows our thoughts and our heartbeat.

If you were to make a guess of the amount of hair on your head, how much would you say it is?

Can't count it, right?

Matthew 10:30 says, *"And even the very hairs of your head are all numbered."* This speaks of a God who knows everything about you. He cares about the amount of hair on your head. But you are only going to know what He says by reading His word.

To meditate is to deeply think about what God has said to you from His word.

1. Psalm 119:15, *"I meditate on your precepts and consider your ways."*
2. Psalm 119:27, *"Cause me to understand the way of your precepts, that I may meditate on your wonderful deeds."*
3. Psalm 1:2, *"But whose delight is in the law of the LORD, and who meditates on his law day and night."*
4. Psalm 143:5, *"I remember the days of long ago; I meditate on all your works and consider what your hands have done."*

SCRIPTURE READING CHALLENGE: Psalm 119

THINGS LEARNED DURING Meditation

Secret Place

My prayer life is based on scripture. A place away from everyone...

> "But when you pray, go into your room, close the door and pray to your Father, who is unseen."
>
> Matthew 6:6

Your secret place is the best place to pour out your heart to the Father. In that secret place is where God revealed Himself to me in profound ways: through visions and revelations.

Do you have that secret place to seek God? *It doesn't always have to be a bedroom, but a place away from everything and everyone.*

As a teenager, my secret place was the *toilet.*

Yes! The toilet.

Growing up in a home that was small and always packed, the toilet was my sacred place to meet with God daily. I would pray, cry out to Him, and read His word. Now as an adult, the toilet is still one of my secret places, along with the bedroom, or the living room when no one is around.

- Moses was tending sheep on his ***own*** in the <u>wilderness</u> when he heard the voice of God speaking from a burning bush.
- Elijah was standing ***alone*** on a <u>mountain</u> when he heard the Lord's whisper in the wind.
- John was ***imprisoned*** on a <u>remote island</u> when he heard the voice of Jesus inviting him to write the last revelation of scripture.

Find your secret place and pour out your heart.

Seclusion is a Good Thing

In your relationship with God, seclusion can be a good

thing.

We can seclude ourselves in God's presence. This involves dropping everything that is going on in your life and taking intentional time to be with God, alone, and undisturbed.

BE INTENTIONAL ABOUT:
- Your devotional life
- Prayer
- Worshiping God
- Serving God
- Living a holy life
- Obeying His word
- Listening to God

This is all part of having a personal relationship with Him.

Your relationship with God should be the first priority, it sets the foundation for your life. *"Seek first his kingdom and his righteousness."*

> "I love those who love me, and those who seek me find me."
>
> Proverbs 8:17

JESUS ISOLATED HIMSELF TO BE WITH HIS FATHER.

I think it is so profound that Jesus did not **need** to spend time away with God because He is the son of God. He was a sinless man, who didn't need to pray, and yet He did.

Jesus did not need to confess any wrongdoing, yet He went away to be with His Father. What a perfect example we have.

Are you getting the picture here?

Men who have a heart for God and a desire to hear Him, to please Him, to love Him, and to be on fire for Him, make time to spend with Him.

Scriptures

As you read these scriptures, I encourage you to apply them in your personal lives and current situations. Let them be your prayer to God. Grow in your relationship with Him.

1. "Call to me and I will answer you and tell you great and unsearchable things you do not know." **Jeremiah 33:3**
2. "As the deer pants for streams of water, so my soul pants for you, my God. My soul thirsts for God, for the living God. When can I go and meet with God?" **Psalm 42:1-2**
3. "How lovely is your dwelling place, Lord Almighty! My soul yearns, even faints, for the courts of the Lord…" **Psalm 84:1-2**
4. "Come near to God and he will come near to you." **James 4:8**
5. "My heart says of you, 'Seek his face!' Your face, Lord, I will seek." **Psalm 27:8**

Those are just a few scriptures that drove me to God and helped to encourage my desire for Him as I prayed.

One scripture in particular that moved me forward was the story of Jacob, as told in Genesis 32:22-30.

"That night Jacob got up and took his two wives, his two female servants and his eleven sons and crossed the ford of the Jabbok. After he had sent them across the stream, he sent over all his possessions. So Jacob was left alone, and a man wrestled with him till daybreak. When the man saw that he could not overpower him, he touched the socket of Jacob's hip so that his hip was wrenched as he wrestled with the man. Then the man said, 'Let me go, for it is daybreak.'

But Jacob replied, 'I will not let you go unless you bless me.'

The man asked him, 'What is your name?"

'Jacob,' he answered.

Then the man said, 'Your name will no longer be Jacob, but Israel, because you have struggled with God and with humans and have overcome.'

Jacob said, 'Please tell me your name.'

But he replied, 'Why do you ask my name?' Then he blessed him there.

So Jacob called the place Peniel, saying, 'It is because I saw God face to face, and yet my life was spared.'"

Jacob was going through a tough time in his life where his brother wanted to kill him, so he left with his wives, children, and possessions. Sometimes we have to wrestle with God. When life hits you so hard and you feel like you can't get up, turn to God in whatever state you are in.

My mom passed away on January 2, 2022. It was the most devastating news I have ever heard in my life. I was crushed, broken, and hurt. I don't think that I have words to describe how I felt that Sunday evening.

To this day I am still in shock and can't believe that she is gone. Her passing rocked my world. The hardest thing was spending time with God because I felt like He didn't come through for me this time. I was angry at my mom for just leaving me and angry at God because deep down I know that He could have saved her.

It was tough doing my devotions because I couldn't bring my mom back. I would still talk with God every day and ask all the whys and hows. I didn't get an answer to the whys. I knew what His word said, "that he is closest to those who are crushed in spirit and broken..." But I felt like God was far from me.

Prayer was hard for me at one point. For months, my prayer time consisted of crying every day and every night. I was so broken that all I could do was go on everyday knowing that I couldn't continue like that.

I couldn't open my mouth to worship because it broke me inside, to know the woman that I love and would do or give anything for was gone; not to be seen physically again. I knew one day at the resurrection I would meet her again, but I wanted her here now.

Why am I saying this?

I knew with all the pain I was feeling, the brokenness, the despair, that God was the only one who understood how I felt. I knew that He was the only one who could comfort me.

One morning, I got up and just worshiped God; screaming with everything that was within me.

I know that God is all powerful, SOVEREIGN and He has everything under control.

~Kimberly Rodriguez

Reminder

Many times, we are struggling with our lives and we run from God instead of running to Him. I encourage you to run to Him first; He knows best.

I rather struggle with God than be alone in this world without His presence and peace.

Confession

Sin separates us from the presence of God.

"God, I realized that in order for me to be free I need to be truthful with myself. I had to come to terms that I need You now more than ever. I realize that I have to let go of who I am and let You take complete control of me. By letting go, I know for sure that my healing will take place because I know that healing is mine through Jesus Christ.

Firstly, God please forgive me; forgive me for not loving others the way I should, forgive me for hating others, forgive me for my lack of self-control, forgive me for my disobedience, for lying, for complaining, forgive me for lusting… but mostly forgive me for my heart not being in the right place with You. I'm sorry. I made a decision to let go of the past, those who have hurt me; the loneliness, sadness and the bitterness that I was feeling on the inside, and the feeling of wanting to destroy things… Where my mind and heart feels trapped, set me free God. But Lord, sometimes I do feel hurt, sad, and lonely. When I do feel *like this, please remind me that I always have You at my side and in my heart."*

That was my conversation with God.

John 8:36, "So if the Son sets you free, you will be free indeed."

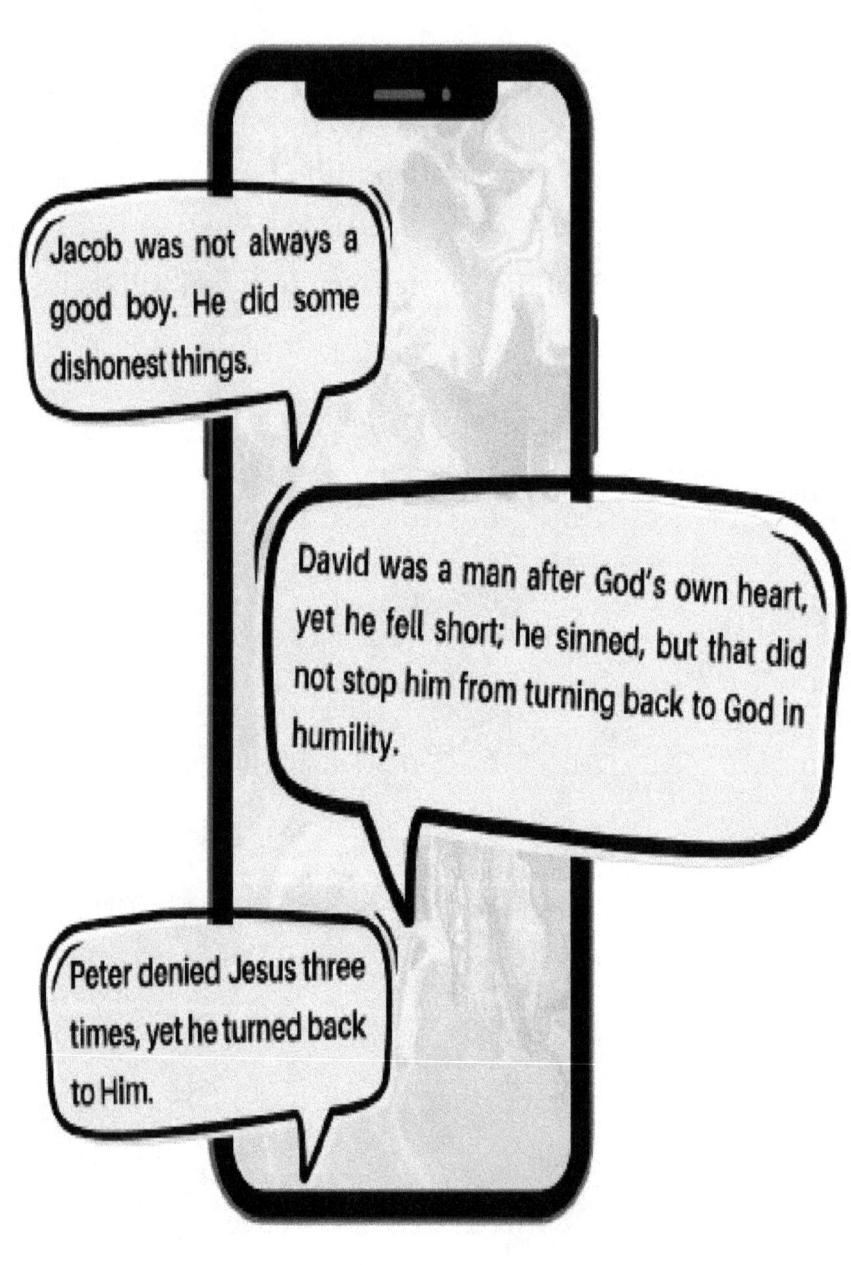

There was a time in my life I was not in the presence of God... My life was **miserable**. I occasionally read the Bible, but prayer was an afterthought. I felt that I could not go to God.

I was too ashamed and guilty. Pride got in the way. Until one night the Holy Spirit was tugging at my heart and it broke me. That night I cried out in the presence of God and I used that scripture and prayed, *"God, I will not let you go until you heal me, until you restore me, and until I have encountered you."*

It was not just that night, but a constant prayer in my life. I would sit in the presence of God, not saying anything. And as simple as it may sound, my life changed.

Remember, at the beginning of this book, I said *talking to God is like talking to your best friend or someone you enjoy talking to.*

Would you pour out your heart to your best friend? Tell them your shortcomings and sins? In most cases, the answer would more than likely be **yes**.

Another part of getting personal with God is telling Him about those sins and your shortcomings. Even though He already knows them, the Bible tells us in 1 John 1:9, *"If we confess our sins, He is faithful and righteous to forgive us our sins and to cleanse us from all unrighteousness."*

SIN AND HOLINESS CANNOT DWELL IN THE SAME PLACE.

We cannot expect God to hear us if we are living a life of sin and not confessing it to Him.

WHEN WE SIN, WE HAVE AN ADVOCATE.

"My dear children, I write this to you so that you will not sin. But if anybody does sin, we have an advocate with the Father— Jesus Christ, the Righteous One."

1 John 2:1

WE ALL FALL SHORT OF THE GLORY OF GOD.

Sin is our biggest downfall. As a Christian, my life was not perfect, and it still isn't. I struggled with sin. You name it, I struggled and battled with it. Sometimes it was the same sin I struggled with. I was tired of going to God with the same sin.

How foolish was I to think that I could not go to Him?

Who else did I expect to run to with my sin?

When sin is in someone's life, it pulls them away from the presence of God. It **DRAGS** them through the **dirt** and burdens them so they feel as if it's impossible to move in order to reach God.

The good thing is that we don't need to go anywhere to confess our sin or to reach out to God. We can reach out to Him right in our messy state.

Trust me, I know what it is to be in a state that I thought was impossible for God to take me out of. I know for a fact that I could not free myself from that bondage.

 **The Prodigal Son** (Luke 15:11-32 NIV)

"Jesus continued: There was a man who had two sons. The younger one said to his father, 'Father, give me my share of the estate.' So he divided his property between them.

Not long after that, the younger son got together all he had, set off for a distant country and there squandered his wealth in wild living. After he had spent everything, there was a severe famine in that whole country, and he began to be in need. So he went and hired himself out to a citizen of that country, who sent him to his fields to feed pigs. He longed to fill his stomach with the pods that the pigs were eating, but no one gave him anything.

When he came to his senses, he said, 'How many of my father's hired servants have food to spare, and here I am starving to death! I will set out and go back to my father and say to him: Father, I have sinned against heaven and against you. I am no longer worthy to be called your son; make me like one of your hired servants.' So he got up and went to his father.

But while he was still a long way off, his father saw him and was filled with compassion for him; he ran to his son, threw his arms around him and kissed him.

The son said to him, 'Father, I have sinned against heaven and against you. I am no longer worthy to be called your son.'

But the father said to his servants, 'Quick! Bring the best robe and put it on him. Put a ring on his finger and sandals on his feet. Bring the fattened calf and kill it. Let's have a feast and celebrate. For this son of mine was dead and is alive again; he was lost and is found.' So they began to celebrate.

Meanwhile, the older son was in the field. When he came near the house, he heard music and dancing. So he called one of the servants and asked him what was going on. 'Your brother has come,' he replied, 'and your father has killed the fattened calf because he has him back safe and sound.'

The older brother became angry and refused to go in. So his father went out and pleaded with him. But he answered his father, 'Look! All these years I've been slaving for you and never disobeyed your orders. Yet you never gave me even a young goat so I could celebrate with my friends. But when this son of yours who has squandered your property with prostitutes comes home, you kill the fattened calf for him!'

'My son,' the father said, 'you are always with me, and everything I have is yours. But we had to celebrate and be glad, because this brother of yours was dead and is alive again; he was lost and is found.'"

What is your story?

- Are you the one who left and still doubt God's acceptance?
- Are you the one who is going to church and doing all the things you are supposed to do, but in your heart, you are that lost son or daughter?

Make that decision today to turn back to Him.

To those of who don't know Him, you can take this opportunity (if you want) to accept Him into your life and have that life changing experience. He is waiting for you. You can have a personal relationship with Him.

I was once just like you: lost and confused, but wanted change. I was that person who was in church religiously, but my heart was far away from God. I was that person who was so caught up in sin and left the church because I wanted to do my own thing.

At one point, I came to my senses that this life is not for me. If this is you, the lost son or daughter, or someone who does not know Jesus Christ as your Lord and Savior, pray this with me...

"Lord, I have not given You my all. I've worshiped you with my lips, but my heart has been far away from You. I have done everything that is wrong in Your eyesight. I blamed You for not caring about me and I turned away from You. I have sinned against You, only You Lord. But today, I am making that decision to know You, I am making that decision to return to You. Forgive me of my sins, come into my life, and be the Lord and Savior my life. Amen."

If you said that prayer and meant it welcome back home, I rejoice with you.

If you said that prayer for the first time, welcome into the family of God, I rejoice with heaven and you.

What is the next step you may ask?

Find a church that preaches sound doctrine, reach out to a Christian friend, or school teacher.

Some things that I struggled with were:

Lust

Pornography

Lying

Deception

Smoking

Stealing

Masturbation

Hatred

> *God, I cannot continue living a lukewarm life. One minute I am on fire for You and the next I am like a fish out of water because I am not living in Your presence. I am relying on my strength to take me through.*

> "Blessed is the one whose transgressions are forgiven, whose sins are covered. Blessed is the one whose sin the Lord does not count against them and in whose spirit is no deceit..."
>
> Psalm 32:1-2

The moment of confession and acknowledgment of sin, God forgives. My bones wasted away, His hands were heavy upon me, my strength was gone, my heart grew weary.

There was defilement, a sin that God could not just let slide.

Sin is deadly.

It is like a venomous snake; once bitten it can take you down.

The venom goes through every vessel
↓
every vein
↓
every cell.

The poison starts to break down everything that is healthy and good in your body.

So does sin.

CHRISTIANS IN THIS GENERATION DON'T FEAR GOD; THERE IS NO FEAR OF GOD IN THE CHURCH.

Our life reflects who we are.

FORGIVENESS

Forgiveness is necessary in a Christian's life. Unforgiveness holds us captive as a slave: to bitterness and hatred. Unforgiveness damages your heart and mind, it keeps you from moving forward. We have heard the saying, *"forgiveness is for you and not the other person."* I never really understood that until I refused to forgive those who continuously hurt me.

THE BIBLE SAID, "IF YOU HATE ANYONE IT IS LIKE YOU HAVE COMMITTED A MURDER."

These things were difficult to admit to myself.

***Sit down and pour out my heart, beg God for forgiveness, and ask Him to change me?** HA! That was an implausible concept to me…*

However, I realized that I no longer wanted to live a sinful life.

Spirit Vs. Flesh

War is **REAL**. And each one of us go through a constant daily battle. Our spirit and flesh battle it out to see which one would have dominance over us. Whichever one we feed the most, that is the one that is going to get BIGGER and *stronger*.

For physical strength we need sleep and food.

Spiritually we need the word of God.

What happens when we don't eat? *We become weak until we eat.*

In the same manner, our spirit needs nourishment to be strong and help us fight temptations.

What happens when our spirit is not being fed? *We feed ourselves with things of this world: music, movies, and ungodly connections...* When we don't feed our spirit with the things of God, it is easy to fall into temptation.

THOUGH JESUS WAS THE SON OF GOD, HE WAS ALSO HUMAN.

Jesus:

- Had flesh just like you and I.
- Overcame the same temptations that we are faced with.
- Fed His spirit daily.
- Made time to spend with His Father. He would always slip away to be with His Father.

> **"For we do not have a high priest who is unable to empathize with our weaknesses, but we have one who has been tempted in every way, just as we are—yet he did not sin."**
>
> **Hebrews 4:15**

Jesus prayed, *"Father let your WILL be DONE in my Life."*

What is the will of God for your life? *The will of God for your life is found in His word and you are only going to understand it by having a personal relationship with Him.*

Can you pray that prayer and say, *"Father, let Your will be done in my life?"* It is not a simple or easy prayer; it is a prayer that breaks you; that makes you die to self, your will, and your desires.

Sometimes our will and desires are totally opposite to the WILL of God.

As Christians, we are not perfect and we are not always kind to others. God is continually molding and shaping us. Being a Christian means surrendering all that you have, giving to God all that you are, in exchange for a changed life. This changed life is not going to happen overnight, it is going to take time.

Think about your life as clay in the potter's hand.

Shaping and molding takes time.

Ladies, the vase or big flower pot that you saw in the variety store, did not happen overnight. It took hours.

Guys, your favorite mug took time to make.

God is going to take His time with you...

Jeremiah 18:1-10,

> "This is the word that came to Jeremiah from the Lord: 'Go down to the potter's house, and there I will give you my message.' So I went down to the potter's house, and I saw him working at the

wheel. But the pot he was shaping from the clay was marred in his hands; so the potter formed it into another pot, shaping it as seemed best to him.

Then the word of the Lord came to me. He said, 'Can I not do with you, Israel, as this potter does?' declares the Lord. 'Like clay in the hand of the potter, so are you in my hand, Israel. If at any time I announce that a nation or kingdom is to be uprooted, torn down and destroyed, and if that nation I warned repents of its evil, then I will relent and not inflict on it the disaster I had planned. And if at another time I announce that a nation or kingdom is to be built up and planted, and if it does evil in my sight and does not obey me, then I will reconsider the good I had intended to do for it.'"

EACH PERSON GREW UP WITH A CERTAIN MINDSET WHICH DICTATED THE CHOICES THEY MADE.

When you become a Christian, Christ has to reshape you to be like Him. God puts you on the wheel of molding and that's where He begins His work in you. You can trust Him to complete the work that He started in you.

> "Being confident of this, that he who began a good work in you will carry it on to completion until the day of Christ Jesus."
>
> **Philippians 1:6**

How I Felt...

- God was not working in my life.
- I was getting worse instead of better.
- My failures were too much for God to overlook or forgive.
- God had given up on me.
- Plagued. *I had many meltdowns and panic attacks, and my thoughts tormented me for a while.*

Believe me when I say that the moment that I went to God, I felt relieved. I never felt so at home and openly welcomed.

We all have sin in our life that seems hard to admit to God. Have you admitted to yourself the sin that holds you back? The sin is heavy on your heart and mind.

Would you believe me if I say that God loves you unconditionally?

Would you accept that there is nothing that can separate you from the love of God?

"For I am convinced that neither death nor life, neither angels nor demons, neither the present nor the future, nor any powers, neither height nor depth, nor anything else in all creation, will be able to separate us from the love of God that is in Christ Jesus our Lord."

Romans 8:38-39

My heart beats joyfully knowing that there is nothing that can separate me from the love of God. Every day I thank God for the sacrifice He made by sending Jesus Christ to save a wretch like me.

I know I am undeserving of His grace and mercy, but Jesus Christ made that possible and I am forever grateful.

> "I give them eternal life, and they shall never perish; no one will snatch them out of my hand."
>
> **John 10:28**

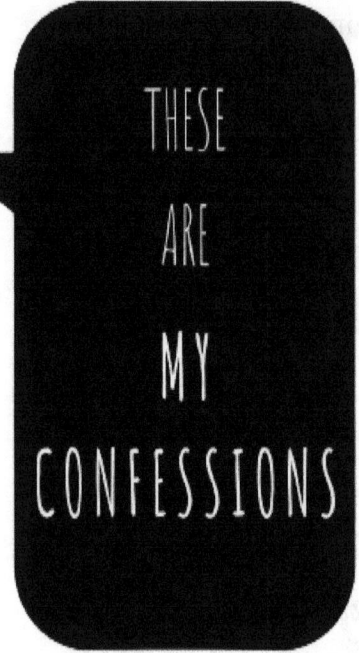

Reading the Word and Praying

A personal relationship with God is more than just going to church. That's not enough!

Going to Bible study is **not** enough if you do not have a personal relationship with God.

I have seen and heard of people who are avid Bible readers and can quote scriptures from Genesis to Revelation, but have <u>**NO**</u> relationship with Jesus Christ.

Following Christ is more than saying the sinner's prayer; it's more than being baptized in water. It is more than saying you go to church with your parents because their parents took them. This is a personal lifelong journey with Christ, giving Him full access to your life. It is impossible to grow spiritually without spending time with God and in His word daily for yourself.

Hearing scriptures on Sundays or Saturdays, or during Bible study, listening to messages on the radio or television, is not going to be enough for your spiritual growth.

DON'T JUST SETTLE FOR READING THE BIBLE AND PRAYING...

I have already made up my mind that *I will serve God for the rest of my life*. Saying this is not an easy statement because serving Christ is not easy, but it is definitely worth it.

Don't fill your days with religious activities and never experience the presence of God, the lover of your soul.

"If all you have is the presence of God, then you have everything in this life."

"The biggest blessing you can ever have is the presence of God."

In my early years as a Christian, I found my devotional time to be considered a routine. I did the same thing every morning and night for two years. At times, I would become so busy involved in ministry that I neglected to read my Bible or pray. In other words, I was doing things for God, but not spending that quality time with Him.

Eventually, my Christian walk was filled with many trials and challenges that I didn't understand. I had no other choice but to rely on God, and I began spending quality time with God and becoming more intimate with Him. I realized that God sometimes allow things to happen in our lives for us to see that it's not only important to do things for Him, but also to build a closer relationship with Him.

My devotional time consisted of meditation, singing, Bible reading, journaling, and praying. Each time was different, and this is where I felt God's unconditional love for me. In these times, He will speak to me and reassure me that He matters the most even during the chaos all around me. These quiet times where I speak, and He listens and vice versa are the best and what I will continue to long for. My devotional time helped me know who God is and who I am because of Him.

I saw that being intentional about my devotional time with God can resist the urge of it becoming a routine. I will encourage anyone reading this to cherish these special moments with God because without Him we cannot do anything. He is the one that gives us our "nourishment" to do whatever He has called us to do.

~ Vernoma Joseph

The Journey

The journey has only now begun for you and me. Press forward in this journey of knowing God personally.

Jesus Christ is my Ark; my safe place. The more I read scriptures, the more my eyes were open to things, the more I cried out to God to change this vessel and make it more like His Son.

I fail so many times. Even in my struggles, I ask myself if I'm struggling with this sin or allowing it and taking the grace of God for granted.

My fear has always been *not serving God*.

I knew when I fell years ago, I did not see myself ever serving God because to me I was too deep in sin. But when I made the decision to go back to God, for the first time I truly understood GRACE and His MERCY.

That scripture that says *if you hear his voice do not harden your heart*; it was my second chance.

He is the God of chances.

That's how much He cares about you and me.

To the person reading this...

You are not alone

You are not worthless

You are not trash

You are not what you think of yourself.

I hope this book helps you realize that you mean more to God than anything in this world. Get to know Him personally. God can help you become who He wants you to be. Hold on as if your life depends on it...

I believe that everyone's devotional life is unique. Therefore, I did not write this book to tell you ***how*** to do your devotions or <u>**how**</u> the presence of God feels.

I wrote it so that you can seek God, encounter Him for yourself, and walk with Him daily. If I were to instruct you, it would be a routine and not something that is special.

I hope this devotional book encourages you to write your personal encounters with God. You will be able to look back at the progress that you have made on this journey.

Pray and ask God for a message every day and how you can apply this message to your life. Then pray that the will of God through His message, will be done in your life.

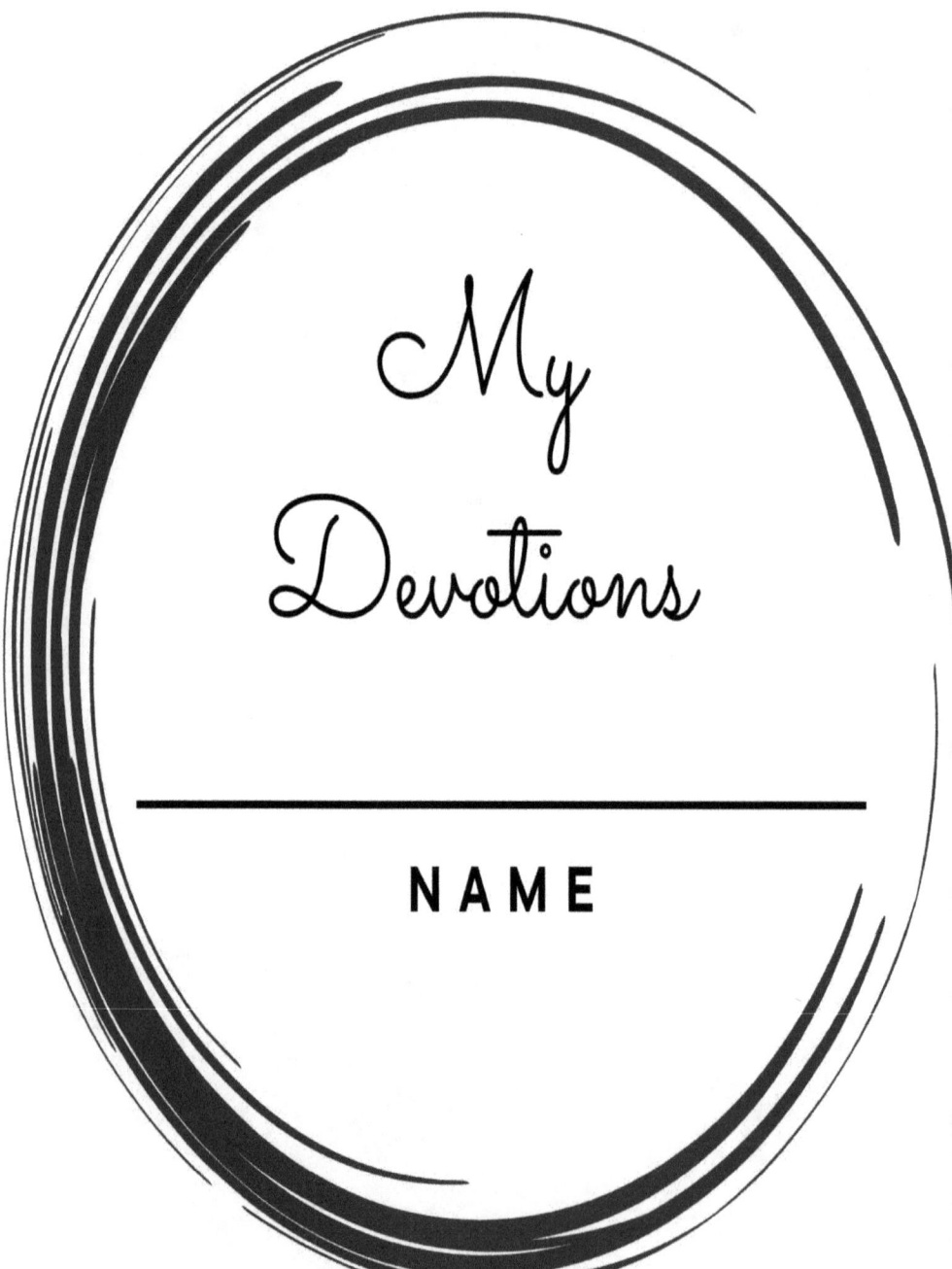

DATE: _____

"Let us come before him with thanksgiving and extol him with music and song."

Psalm 95:2

MESSAGE
What is God saying to me today?

APPLICATION
How can I apply this message to my life?

faith
PRAYER

Date: _____

"Where can I go from your Spirit? Where can I flee from your presence?"

Psalm 139:7

MESSAGE
What is God saying to me today?

APPLICATION
How can I apply this message to my life?

faith
PRAYER

DATE: _____

"Now the Lord is the Spirit, and where the Spirit of the Lord is, there is freedom."

2 Corinthians 3:17

MESSAGE
What is God saying to me today?

APPLICATION
How can I apply this message to my life?

PRAYER

DATE: _____

"I say to the Lord, 'You are my Lord; apart from you I have no good thing.'"

Psalm 16:2

MESSAGE
What is God saying to me today?

APPLICATION
How can I apply this message to my life?

faith
PRAYER

DATE: _____

"Then Moses said to him, 'If your Presence does not go with us, do not send us up from here.'"

Exodus 33:15

MESSAGE
What is God saying to me today?

APPLICATION
How can I apply this message to my life?

PRAYER

DATE: _____

"But as for me, it is good to be near God. I have made the Sovereign Lord my refuge; I will tell of all your deeds."

Psalm 73:28

MESSAGE
What is God saying to me today?

APPLICATION
How can I apply this message to my life?

faith
PRAYER

DATE: _____

"For through him we both have access to the Father by one Spirit."

Ephesians 2:18

MESSAGE
What is God saying to me today?

APPLICATION
How can I apply this message to my life?

faith
PRAYER

DATE: _____

"Do not cast me from your presence or take your Holy Spirit from me."

Psalm 51:11

MESSAGE
What is God saying to me today?

APPLICATION
How can I apply this message to my life?

faith
PRAYER

DATE: _____

> "Repent, then, and turn to God, so that your sins may be wiped out, that times of refreshing may come from the Lord..."
>
> Acts 3:19

MESSAGE
What is God saying to me today?

APPLICATION
How can I apply this message to my life?

faith
PRAYER

DATE: _____

"Humble yourselves before the Lord, and he will lift you up."

James 4:10

MESSAGE
What is God saying to me today?

APPLICATION
How can I apply this message to my life?

faith
PRAYER

DATE: _____

> "In the same way, I tell you, there is rejoicing in the presence of the angels of God over one sinner who repents."
>
> Luke 15:10

MESSAGE
What is God saying to me today?

APPLICATION
How can I apply this message to my life?

PRAYER

DATE: _____

"Humble yourselves, therefore, under God's mighty hand, that he may lift you up in due time."

1 Peter 5:6

MESSAGE
What is God saying to me today?

APPLICATION
How can I apply this message to my life?

PRAYER

DATE: _____

"Submit yourselves, then, to God. Resist the devil, and he will flee from you."

James 4:7

MESSAGE
What is God saying to me today?

APPLICATION
How can I apply this message to my life?

faith PRAYER

DATE: _____

"Take my yoke upon you and learn from me, for I am gentle and humble in heart, and you will find rest for your souls."

Matthew 11:29

MESSAGE
What is God saying to me today?

APPLICATION
How can I apply this message to my life?

faith
PRAYER

DATE: _____

"Therefore, whoever takes the lowly position of this child is the greatest in the kingdom of heaven."

Matthew 18:4

MESSAGE
What is God saying to me today?

APPLICATION
How can I apply this message to my life?

faith
PRAYER

DATE: _____

"I will glory in the Lord; let the afflicted hear and rejoice."

Psalm 34:2

MESSAGE
What is God saying to me today?

APPLICATION
How can I apply this message to my life?

faith

PRAYER

DATE: _____

"He guides the humble in what is right and teaches them his way."

Psalm 25:9

MESSAGE
What is God saying to me today?

APPLICATION
How can I apply this message to my life?

PRAYER

DATE: _____

"Therefore, get rid of all moral filth and the evil that is so prevalent and humbly accept the word planted in you, which can save you."

James 1:21

MESSAGE
What is God saying to me today?

APPLICATION
How can I apply this message to my life?

PRAYER

DATE: _____

"Look to the Lord and his strength; seek his face always."

1 Chronicles 16:11

MESSAGE
What is God saying to me today?

APPLICATION
How can I apply this message to my life?

PRAYER

DATE: _____

"Now devote your heart and soul to seeking the LORD your God. Begin to build the sanctuary of the LORD God…"

1 Chronicles 22:19

MESSAGE
What is God saying to me today?

APPLICATION
How can I apply this message to my life?

faith

PRAYER

DATE: _____

"God did this so that they would seek him and perhaps reach out for him and find him, though he is not far from any one of us."

Acts 17:27

MESSAGE
What is God saying to me today?

APPLICATION
How can I apply this message to my life?

faith
PRAYER

DATE: _____

"Come near to God and he will come near to you."

James 4:8

MESSAGE
What is God saying to me today?

APPLICATION
How can I apply this message to my life?

faith
PRAYER

DATE: _____

"You will seek me and find me when you seek me with all your heart."

Jeremiah 29:13

MESSAGE
What is God saying to me today?

APPLICATION
How can I apply this message to my life?

PRAYER

DATE: _____

> "But seek first his kingdom and his righteousness, and all these things will be given to you as well."
>
> Matthew 6:33

MESSAGE
What is God saying to me today?

APPLICATION
How can I apply this message to my life?

faith PRAYER

DATE: _____

"I love those who love me, and those who seek me find me."

Proverbs 8:17

MESSAGE
What is God saying to me today?

APPLICATION
How can I apply this message to my life?

faith
PRAYER

DATE: _____

"Those who know your name trust in you, for you, LORD, have never forsaken those who seek you."

Psalm 9:10

MESSAGE
What is God saying to me today?

APPLICATION
How can I apply this message to my life?

faith
PRAYER

DATE: _____

"The LORD looks down from heaven on all mankind to see if there are any who understand, any who seek God."

Psalm 14:2

MESSAGE
What is God saying to me today?

APPLICATION
How can I apply this message to my life?

faith
PRAYER

DATE: _____

"The lions may grow weak and hungry, but those who seek the LORD lack no good thing."

Psalm 34:10

MESSAGE
What is God saying to me today?

APPLICATION
How can I apply this message to my life?

faith
PRAYER

DATE: _____

"But may all who seek you rejoice and be glad in you; may those who long for your saving help always say, 'The LORD is great!'"

Psalm 40:16

MESSAGE
What is God saying to me today?

APPLICATION
How can I apply this message to my life?

PRAYER

DATE: _____

"You, God, are my God, earnestly I seek you; I thirst for you, my whole being longs for you, in a dry and parched land where there is no water."

Psalm 63:1

MESSAGE
What is God saying to me today?

APPLICATION
How can I apply this message to my life?

faith
PRAYER

DATE: _____

"Seek the LORD while he may be found; call upon him while he is near."

Isaiah 55:6-7

MESSAGE
What is God saying to me today?

APPLICATION
How can I apply this message to my life?

faith
PRAYER

DATE: _____

"My heart says of you, 'Seek his face!' Your face, LORD, I will seek."

Psalm 27:8

MESSAGE
What is God saying to me today?

APPLICATION
How can I apply this message to my life?

faith
PRAYER

DATE: _____

"The poor will see and be glad— you who seek God, may your hearts live!"

Psalm 69:32

MESSAGE
What is God saying to me today?

APPLICATION
How can I apply this message to my life?

PRAYER

DATE: _____

"Glory in his holy name; let the heart of those who seek the LORD rejoice."

1 Chronicles 16:10

MESSAGE
What is God saying to me today?

APPLICATION
How can I apply this message to my life?

faith
PRAYER

DATE: _____

"Shout it aloud, do not hold back."

Isaiah 58:1

MESSAGE
What is God saying to me today?

APPLICATION
How can I apply this message to my life?

faith
PRAYER

DATE: _____

"I sought the LORD, and he answered me; he delivered me from all my fears."

Psalm 34:4

MESSAGE
What is God saying to me today?

APPLICATION
How can I apply this message to my life?

faith
PRAYER

DATE: _____

"But if I were you, I would appeal to God; I would lay my cause before him."

Job 5:8

MESSAGE
What is God saying to me today?

APPLICATION
How can I apply this message to my life?

faith
PRAYER

DATE: _____

"May these words of my mouth and this meditation of my heart be pleasing in your sight, LORD, my Rock and my Redeemer."

Psalm 19:14

MESSAGE
What is God saying to me today?

APPLICATION
How can I apply this message to my life?

PRAYER

DATE: _____

"May my meditation be pleasing to him; as I rejoice in the LORD."

Psalm 104:34

MESSAGE
What is God saying to me today?

APPLICATION
How can I apply this message to my life?

PRAYER

DATE: _____

"Reflect on what I am saying, for the Lord will give you insight into all this."

2 Timothy 2:7

MESSAGE
What is God saying to me today?

APPLICATION
How can I apply this message to my life?

faith
PRAYER

DATE: _____

"I keep my eyes always on the LORD. With him at my right hand, I will not be shaken."

Psalm 16:8

MESSAGE
What is God saying to me today?

APPLICATION
How can I apply this message to my life?

faith
PRAYER

DATE: _____

"On my bed I remember you; I think of you through the watches of the night."

Psalm 63:6

MESSAGE
What is God saying to me today?

APPLICATION
How can I apply this message to my life?

faith
PRAYER

DATE: _____

"I meditate on your precepts and consider your ways. I delight in your decrees; I will not neglect your word."

Psalm 119:15-16

MESSAGE
What is God saying to me today?

APPLICATION
How can I apply this message to my life?

PRAYER

DATE: _____

"Keep this Book of the Law on your lips; meditate on it day and night..."

Joshua 1:8

MESSAGE
What is God saying to me today?

APPLICATION
How can I apply this message to my life?

faith PRAYER

DATE: _____

"I will consider all your works and meditate on all your mighty deeds."

Psalm 77:12

MESSAGE
What is God saying to me today?

APPLICATION
How can I apply this message to my life?

PRAYER

DATE: _____

> "Great are the works of the LORD; they are pondered by all who delight in them."
>
> **Psalm 111:2**

MESSAGE
What is God saying to me today?

APPLICATION
How can I apply this message to my life?

PRAYER

DATE: _____

"I will praise the LORD, who counsels me; even at night my heart instructs me."

Psalm 16:7

MESSAGE
What is God saying to me today?

APPLICATION
How can I apply this message to my life?

faith
PRAYER

DATE: _____

"Accept instruction from his mouth and lay up his words in your heart."

Job 22:22

MESSAGE
What is God saying to me today?

APPLICATION
How can I apply this message to my life?

PRAYER

DATE: _____

"I have hidden your word in my heart that I might not sin against you."

Psalm 119:11

MESSAGE
What is God saying to me today?

APPLICATION
How can I apply this message to my life?

PRAYER

DATE: _____

"In the night, LORD, I remember your name, that I may keep your law."

Psalm 119:55

MESSAGE
What is God saying to me today?

APPLICATION
How can I apply this message to my life?

faith
PRAYER

DATE: _____

"Tremble and do not sin; when you are on your beds, search your hearts and be silent."

Psalm 4:4

MESSAGE
What is God saying to me today?

APPLICATION
How can I apply this message to my life?

faith PRAYER

www.ingramcontent.com/pod-product-compliance
Lightning Source LLC
Chambersburg PA
CBHW070647160426
43194CB00009B/1618